A Passion for Blue & White

A Passion for Blue & White

Carolyne Roehm

Broadway Books
New York

This book is dedicated to my mentor Oscar de la Renta,
who as a boss made work so much fun, as a
teacher taught me so many things
beyond the world of fashion, and as a friend
has supported me through thick and thin.
Thank you, dear Oscar, for giving me so very much.
—Carolyne

Living

Blue and white has been a constant in my interior design work, from my first bachelorette pad to an enormous house on the beach. I have always been inspired by nature, and no other combination is as omnipresent as glorious blue and white in all its tints and hues.

Page 13

Entertaining

Flowers and food look fabulous on tables decorated with blue and white. The endless assortment of dishes, glassware, and linens available in this bold combination enables the hostess to create beautiful tables for every season, occasion, and budget.

Page 117

From the Garden

White flowers abound, and glorious delphinium, hydrangeas, and bachelor buttons are the most brilliant blue blossoms. The way other colors from the garden pop when arranged in a blue-and-white vase makes it inspiring to create endless bouquets with surefire style and ease.

Page 167

Collecting

Blue and white is an artful color motif evident in more cultures than any other. The Chinese, Moors, Dutch, French, English, Portuguese, Swedish, and Persian cultures have created ceramics, textiles, paints, and glass in myriad blues with white throughout history—much to the delight of collectors like me.

Page 215

Elements & Inspiration

A swatch of fabric from France initiated me into the world of design possibilities associated with blue and white. Thus began a lifelong interest in the way this wonderful combination enlivens everything from napkins and drapes to wrapping paper and ribbons.

Page 267

HEN DESIGNERS REVIEW THEIR BODY of work, they often discover motifs or threads that consistently appear throughout their designs. In my case, a love of nature has been a constant source of inspiration, and in particular, nature's quintessential color combination of blue and white never ceases to amaze me. The look of pristine snow against deep blue Aspen skies; spires of blue and white delphinium in a garden; Connecticut's spring mornings where the apple blossoms and nodding heads of white narcissus are in contrast to soft blue skies and vibrant green grass—these and many more images found in nature have informed my work for the last thirty-five years. From fashion to interiors, and tabletop to gardens, the presence of blue and white is a constant in my past collections as well as throughout my previous eight books. It seemed natural that I would eventually do a book on living and designing with this seminal color combination.

From my early twenties, I have lived with, collected, and loved blue and white. While I was getting ready to decorate my first little flat in New York, my mentor Oscar de la Renta showed me a classic blue-and-white fabric from France, inspired by the chateau at Verrières-le-Buisson, where French writer Louise Levêque de Vilmorin was raised. The moment I saw that swatch of lovely fabric, I knew I wanted the apartment to be done from floor to ceiling in it. Alas, I was a young design assistant living on very limited wages and my champagne tastes with my beer budget would not allow me to do as I wished. I was so disappointed that the $35-a-yard fabric, which was a fortune at that time, was way beyond my means. Always full of great ideas, Oscar mentioned that he had done a positive and negative of a blue-and-white print for his line of sheets and that perhaps we could buy the fabric from the mill. One can imagine my glee when I found that the wide sheeting fabric was going to cost me 99 cents a yard! I draped the walls, the chairs, the sofa, and my canopy bed, brought from home, in this ersatz Ferrière.

When you look at nature, you see blue and white everywhere: brilliant blue skies, fluffy white clouds, magical icebergs, blue flowers. This color combination inspires linens, porcelains, embroidery, and this book.

STARTING WITH MY FIRST APARTMENT, THE quest for blue and white in all types of decorative elements began. I scoured flea markets and import stores to find dishes, lamps, and linens to go in my blue-and-white cocoon. Whenever and wherever I traveled, I searched for affordable offerings in blue and white and discovered how many cultures were as much in love with this classic combination as I was. In museums, each country offered up beautiful interpretations: Azulejos from Portugal, Delft from the Netherlands, Chinese porcelain from the famous Ming and Kangxi periods, porcelain created for export from the Far East, fountains of tiles and vessels from Turkey, indigo fabrics from Japan, blue-and-white dhurries from India, faience from France, Wedgwood from England, and Meissen from Saxony. The list was endless. While I could not afford the blue-and-white antiques from around the world, each country made reproductions and new designs for the budding collector.

Many years and lives later, I have a rather large collection of antiques that are much like the ones I fell in love with in my travels. Still, at the time I was purchasing my reproductions, I was as excited as any museum curator with each new piece I added to my blue-and-white nest.

I have consistently loved to design with blue and white. I used it at Weatherstone, my home in Connecticut; in Paris, at an apartment I had; and at Westbury, my place in Aspen. When I rebuilt Weatherstone after a fire, the classic color combination found a place in many of the new interiors. Just as I love to decorate with it, I have done an entire garden of delphinium in various shades of blue, violet, and white, and mixed those towering spires with masses of iceberg roses. As is clear in my previous books, a majority of my decoration for my lunches, dinners, and parties revolves around my collections of blue-and-white china, ceramic dishes, and decorations. This book includes new photos of tables often with the same dishes, but used in a new way.

This brings me to one of the key factors in the popularity of blue and white. In doing additional research, I learned that the passion for this combination is universal. I have read numerous accounts about how the Egyptians thought it signified immortality and power. It was a symbol of prosperity, as few but royalty

Left: This photo taken by Victor Skrebneski for a Carolyne Roehm ad campaign exemplifies my passion for blue and white, from the stripe in the dress that I designed for a Spring 1990 collection to the tiled room done by Vincent Fourcade from an antique panel of Portuguese azulejos. Right: The transition from house to the formal white garden is a veranda decorated in blue and white.

could afford the pigments desired by all. In many cultures and religions, blue is the color for heavenly gods; it represents the spiritual and the divine. In Christianity, it stands for purity; in certain cultures, it is the symbol for fidelity. Blue is restful and calming; white as the symbol of "light" is clean and pure. There are endless stories and historical anecdotes explaining the significance of blue and white, but I think there are several simple reasons why it is so popular. First, it is so prevalent in nature; second, it always looks fresh; and third, it is a palette that works beautifully with just about every color in the spectrum.

For those of you who are interested, there is a plethora of information on the meaning and history of blue and white, and its use in all of the decorative arts. There are many photos of beautiful rooms, houses, galleries, and legendary collections in blue and white. This book is my personal story of designing and living with this magical color combination. I hope in some small way it will inspire you.

—*Carolyne Roehm*

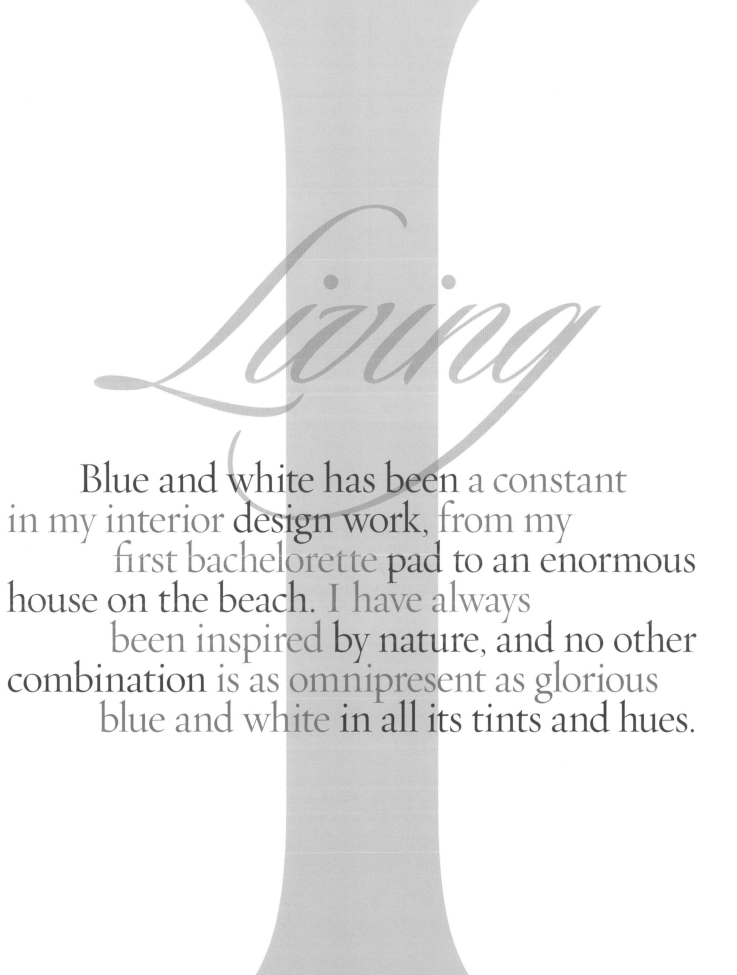

Blue and white has been a constant
in my interior design work, from my
first bachelorette pad to an enormous
house on the beach. I have always
been inspired by nature, and no other
combination is as omnipresent as glorious
blue and white in all its tints and hues.

living with blue & white

My love affair with this classic color combination began with my first blue-and-white apartment in the seventies. Wherever I have lived, I've had rooms in blue and white and collected many decorative pieces in these hues. When I began rebuilding Weatherstone, my house in northwestern Connecticut, after the fire that destroyed it, I knew this perfect pairing would be part of the décor.

The grand staircase at Weatherstone has a clean, simple appeal, which relies on the strength of the architecture. A round table set inside its curve complements its graceful lines and holds a few pieces from my collection that look as striking from above as they do up close.

Mirrors are beautiful in their own right, but they create magic in a room when they catch the reflection of flowers, candlelight, or a beautiful object.

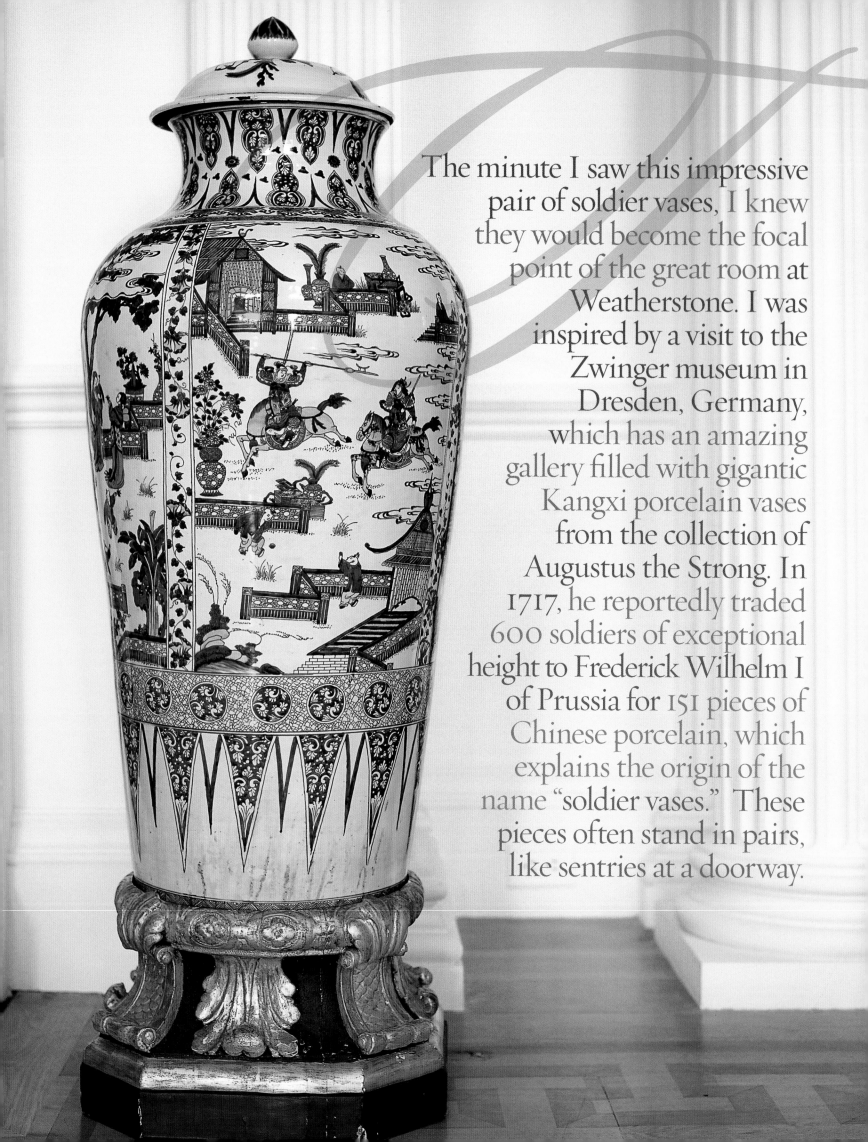

The minute I saw this impressive pair of soldier vases, I knew they would become the focal point of the great room at Weatherstone. I was inspired by a visit to the Zwinger museum in Dresden, Germany, which has an amazing gallery filled with gigantic Kangxi porcelain vases from the collection of Augustus the Strong. In 1717, he reportedly traded 600 soldiers of exceptional height to Frederick Wilhelm I of Prussia for 151 pieces of Chinese porcelain, which explains the origin of the name "soldier vases." These pieces often stand in pairs, like sentries at a doorway.

a touch of blue

Living with blue and white does not mean every surface has to be painted or draped in the combination. How you use these shades depends on the room: Find the blue that works with the space and establish a balance so the color isn't overpowering. The morning room at Weatherstone, for example, is white punctuated with blue accents. Blue evokes such a strong, emotional response in the viewer that sometimes it is most effective in beautiful, small doses.

A verre églomisée mirror in Prussian blue and gold is one of a pair that flanks the fireplace in the morning room at Weatherstone.

THE MORNING ROOM (SO CALLED because the early morning sun bathes the room in light) is a lovely place to sit and read the morning papers and linger over several cups of coffee or tea. The space originally was the dining room of the old house, but on rebuilding Weatherstone, I decided I no longer wanted a large dining room that only looked right and felt inviting if it had a minimum of ten people in it. Nowadays I prefer to have dinners of four to six people, so it seemed like a wasted space, one I merely walked through most of the time.

I made the decision to eliminate the traditional dining room and make this an actual living space with a sofa, chairs, tables, and built-in bookcases to house my books on gardening, design, and architecture. When I wish to give the occasional larger dinner, I move a few pieces out and set up party tables that can seat fifty people. Although the room is white, indigo accents give it a little gravitas and tie all of the different elements in it together. One of the joys of working in a predominantly blue-and-white palette is that all colors look great with it. Blue and white works well as a neutral background for an array of colors.

Touches of gold add a note of polish to the morning room, which blends a sense of formality and comfort in the décor. This blue is a Prussian blue, and I especially like how the shade works so well with gold. The painted blue and white floor of faux stone was inspired by a marble floor in a seventeenth-century château.

A painted blue-and-white eighteenth-century English hunt table has a strong presence in the morning room at Weatherstone. The table, topped with antique globes and white orchids in blue-and-white porcelain, fits neatly into the bow of the bay window. I love unusual shapes in furniture, and while the room was designed around a beautiful Jean-Baptiste Oudry still life, this particular piece complements the painting, which has a hunting theme.

The Prussian blues on the painted floor and in the eighteenth-century tapestry on the chairs play off the tints of the same color in the Oudry painting and give the morning room a cohesive look. I love the blue flowers on these creamy white slippers, which echo the style of patterns throughout the space.

In the morning room, I have three tables in different sizes and shapes, which I move in and out of the room as needed. When I want to use the room for dining, this nineteenth-century table can seat six comfortably, which is my preferred number of guests for a dinner party. The table is set with my favorite blue-and-white eighteenth-century Wedgwood service. The landscape by Jean-Baptiste Pillement is an example of camaïeux, a painting technique that uses a single color or several tints unrealistic to the object or scene represented. In this case, blue was the predominant color (camaïeux bleu); when the technique uses another shade—gray or yellow—the name changes to camaïeux grisaille or camaïeux cirage.

While I admire so many styles and periods, my favorite is the eighteenth century. The decorative arts in Western Europe reached their zenith during this marvelous time period.

Elements and details from the morning room are a mix of French, English, German, Swedish, and Italian pieces. I like how the colors and motifs echo each other—and the subtle way the globes underscore the international references.

The morning room at Weatherstone has beautiful light, and while I painted the walls white to take advantage of it, the room reads blue and white because of the many blue decorative elements. Opposite: During the holiday season, I sometimes stray away from a red-and-green theme and use a blue-and-white color scheme that works surprisingly well with a green wreath or urns filled with narcissus.

Westbury, my Aspen residence, is a place of light with seventy-four large windows bringing nature inside. At night, I light the fireplaces and fill the house with candlelight, making the dining room a magical place to dine.

Having already created one ski house and ranch in Colorado, I wanted Westbury to be different. The inspiration was a Swedish hunting lodge and the cool blues, whites, and grays that look beautiful in a northern climate.

I stained antique trophies white and covered the walls with them to complement the eighteenth-century Swedish furniture in the dining room. They cast beautiful shadows in sunlight or candlelight.

For years I have loved the light, colors, and simplicity of beautiful eighteenth-century Swedish rooms. Westbury is situated in a glorious Aspen grove, surrounded by mountains, and with its many windows, the rooms are filled with extraordinary light that illuminates its Gustavian influences, an eighteenth-century Swedish Neo-classical style of décor.

Westbury is just a bit less formal than Weatherstone and my apartment in New York. Instead of silver and vermeil, the candlesticks, dinnerware, and decorative accessories are all in pewter with horn accents—perfect for the fantasy hunting lodge dining room.

in the kitchen

The kitchen, the breakfast room, and the butler's pantry at Weatherstone are the most used rooms in the house, and that is why I need them to be both practical and cheerful. Classic white beadboard walls and cabinets housing my extensive collection of blue-and-white porcelain, ceramics, and glassware decorate the rooms where guests invariably gather. This is where we cook, eat our casual meals, and arrange flowers—and my dogs sleep on their individual blue-and-white cushions.

I have collected blue-and-white dishes,

Thirty-five years of collecting (even with editing throughout the years) requires ample storage space. I like the old-fashioned glass cupboards, as they display collections that help decorate the room.

accessories, and cobalt glass since the seventies.

Waking up with blue and white puts me in a good mood, especially with a bunch of daisies nearby. Opposite: Another grouping in blue and white, this time for a delicious bowl of soup on a winter's night, while the first signs of spring blossom in cobalt bulb vases.

Sunny and simple: A blue-and-white palette resides comfortably in the kitchen, a room where practicality rules. Striped and checked dishtowels or cobalt blue glassware provide welcome bursts of pattern and color.

Clockwise from top left: Cobalt vases hold bunches of just-picked herbs. Homespun touches—cookies wrapped in a dishtowel, wooden spoons in an English Parian pitcher, a doggy dish of biscuits, striped dishtowels and cobalt bowls—all stand out in blue and white.

a love of indigo

Throughout my life, I've been drawn to the color blue in all of its tonalities. Indigo is a favorite shade I thought would work with two cherished objects I had found for my bedroom when I began rebuilding Weatherstone. From my favorite dealer in London, I obtained a beautiful French mirror and a wonderful Danish clock, both from the eighteenth century. Each is so unusual in design that without another piece of furniture in the room, they define the space and the spirit of it completely.

In practical terms, the Danish clock was an unnecessary piece of furniture in the bedroom, yet from a design perspective, it makes the room. The French eighteenth-century chairs are dressed in a romantic blue-and-white petit point.

For years I longed for this beautiful Swedish mirror.
The maker was Burchardt Precht, a German sculptor
and cabinetmaker who created these amazing cobalt
glass and gilt-gessoed mirrors for Swedish palaces. The
unusual shape and colored glass make it stand out
from the white walls of the upstairs gallery just outside
the master bedroom. Opposite: A blue-and-white
Chinese bowl holds a bouquet of white lilacs.

The ancient Egyptians believed indigo
blue was a symbol of power and
immortality, and long before the advent
of man-made dyes, indigo fabric used
natural blue dyes from sources such as
plants and sea snails. While these are
not the reasons I selected this fabric, I
love the lore. What is also appealing is
the simplicity of the embroidery.

*I wanted a painted eighteenth-century bed for the master bedroom, but
knew from experience that the style would be too narrow for this interior.
From an antique dealer in London I was able to have a reproduction of a
beautiful English bed made to fit the exact proportions needed.*

Mixing objects of different origins and styles can be very effective done in blue and white. Opposite: A look at the fireplace in the master bedroom. The mixing of styles and periods in furniture and accessories in an interior reflects the interests and collections of the owner; this kind of juxtaposition is what makes a house unique.

I have always been more interested in unusual pieces of furniture that you do not see in every antique store—even older pieces that have a great provenance and would be considered museum quality. The originality of a piece is at the forefront of my mind when I'm collecting.

Torchieres, barometers, interesting mirrors, clocks, benches, and stools are not the essentials in a room, but contribute so much in making an interior distinctive and appealing.

in the bedroom

Of all the hues in the color spectrum, both blue and white symbolize peace and calm—a desirable combination for a bedroom. Although many rooms in my homes are decorated in a rather tailored way, the master and guest bedrooms are totally feminine. I have always felt these private areas are a reflection of one's inner life and personality.

The focal point of the bedroom in Manhattan is the Robert Adam fireplace. Adam, one of the preeminent British architects of the eighteenth century, was known for his use of decorative ornamentation on designs with classical proportions. Above the mantle, an eighteenth-century Swedish mirror and English appliqué sconces reside alongside a selection of porcelain flowers from my collection.

Reflected in an eighteenth-
century English mirror
(one of a pair that frames
the bed) is the fireplace.
Opposite: The bed, with its
graceful, curvilinear lines, was
reproduced from a nineteenth-
century model in a cool blue
with golden floral vines.
The walls are covered in the
same fabric as the bed in order
to give the room the feeling
of an inviting cocoon.

F

EMININITY IN MY BEDROOMS IS AN ESSENTIAL PART OF MY decorative lexicon. This is the place I need to feel cozy, secure, and very comfortable. Curling up in a bed covered in beautiful linens is such a wonderful luxury and an important part of my sense of well-being. I do not keep personal photos in the public rooms of the house, but there are many in my bedroom, dressing room, and bath. This is my inner sanctum, where my bedside and dressing tables are filled with images and possessions I love.

In my previous apartment, I had a wonderful lit à la Polonaise, a somewhat grand style of bed that traditionally has a high canopy and bedposts lavishly draped in fabrics. It would not fit under the low ceiling of this bedroom, so I pulled out a clipping of a nineteenth-century upholstered bed I liked and had it reproduced. I upholstered the walls in the same fabric, which makes this private space feel comfortable and enveloping.

Details that share a commonality in color, shape, or texture give a finished look to a space. Train your eye to recognize similarities so a design thread runs throughout to generate a true sense of style in a room.

Cool blue reigns as the presiding color in the bedroom, but hints of white, gold, and brown also make an appearance. Silver accents go beautifully with this blue-violet hue, especially when a cluster of white roses is also in the picture. Purple beads heighten the drama by bringing out the violet undertones. It's clear the eighteenth-century English painter John Wootton understood the impact of white set against a background of blue; his painting beautifully reflects this visual effect.

Westbury is all about light and views. From the bed in the master bedroom, one can gaze out the Palladian window and derive inspiration from the magnificent landscape. It gives one the feeling of living in the tops of the Aspen trees, that grow on the steep mountain behind the house.

I have always admired interior designer Axel Vervoort's dining room in his castle in Belgium. That room filled with miniature Chinese export porcelain on small brackets inspired me to create a similar look in the master bedroom in Colorado. I used larger pieces of blue-and-white Delft and heightened the effect by dressing the bed in a blue-and-white fabric and hanging a white mirror above it that reflects the glistening snow and Aspen's blue skies.

A painting by French Rococo artist Jean-Baptiste Pillement is a beautiful backdrop for my collection of Delft and handmade porcelain flowers. Opposite: The central window has a clear view of nature at its best. Swedish furniture upholstered in stripes heightens the clean lines of the interior.

A window seat in the master bedroom is a perfect place to read and the favorite perch of Floozie the Australian Kelpie, from where she can keep her eye on the elk. Opposite: An eighteenth-century Italian table sits in the central window holding pieces of Delft, Chinese porcelain, and my favorite porcelain flowers.

Ever since my days in fashion, I have always loved mixing prints, patterns, and textures. To combine these different elements effectively, it is important to find a common thread—in this case the colors blue and white in compatible tonalities.

Stripes, checks, a floral jacquard, and the carpet with its blue accents were selected because of their color compatibility with the Jean-Baptiste Pillement painting, which was the inspiration for this Westbury room.

in the bedroom

Guests at Westbury always comment on the joy of opening their eyes to the beauty of the Aspen-covered mountains— whether the trees are glowing in their golden autumn finery, laden with pristine snow, or are just bursting into a delicate spring green. A cozy bedroom in delicate blue is so comfortable that I sometimes cannot get my guests to rise and shine.

The dressing table in the blue guest room is covered in striped silk taffeta and offers a view out to a magnificent mountain.

The delicate blue-gray of the walls is a much more sophisticated color than powder or baby blue. I feel one has to be careful with these light blues, as they can easily become too "sweet." I love the deep red accents that are picked up from the Swedish print used on the bed. Opposite: The pair of side tables were only bases when I found them. I had a carpenter make tops for them and then faux-finished them in what the French call "blanc caisse" or a "broken white" that looks old.

Comfort is the key to a successful guest bedroom—plump pillows, a cozy

There are a few other essentials that make a guest rooom inviting:
a dressing table (if room permits), good-quality hangers,
warm blankets, a reading lamp, an alarm clock, and fluffy towels.

reading chair. Good linens make your guests feel pampered and welcome.

in a guest room

The first guest room I decorated at
Weatherstone was a small one on
the main floor of the old house, and
of course it was in blue and white.
That was twenty-five years ago, before I had
collected very much in those colors.
Still, I love the simplicity of the
striped walls and the eighteenth-century
Chinese Chippendale bed dressed
in a classic French fabric.

*The combination of blue-and-white-checked bed linens and the floral pattern on the
scalloped headers makes the Chinese Chippendale bed feel like a special place. Guests
want to linger over morning coffee brought to them on a breakfast tray.*

It's easy to see the appeal of blue and white in these sweet blossoms on a dark blue tufted backdrop. Opposite: Pristine white cosmos from the cutting garden and frilly Queen Anne's lace make a fresh and simple bouquet in a blue-and-white English Parian ware pitcher.

I learned everything I needed to know about creating an inviting guest room

*An inviting guest room includes water in a pretty carafe
set next to the bed; beautiful linens; fresh flowers; and a place
for ladies to put their make up on with good lighting.*

from the late Françoise de la Renta, who was a person of consummate style.

I have always loved the look of a lit à la Polonaise. It is so romantic, cozy, and protective. This is one I purchased immediately after the fire at Weatherstone, as I didn't have a bed to sleep in, and I certainly needed to feel protected at that time. It was also my bed in the cottage where I stayed during the reconstruction. It now is in the blue-and-white guest room in the main house.

Because of the fire, I decided to close up my apartment in Paris, as I knew I would have to be on site most of the time during the rebuilding of the house. Most of the furnishings for the three guest rooms came from that apartment, and I like to think of this particular shade as Parisian blue.

A breakfast tray has a pleasing effect set in blue and white with a sprig of lily of the valley. The fabric on this painted bench picks up the checks and florals in the room. Opposite: When I am in Paris, I sometimes stop by stalls at the Paris flea market in Saint-Ouen. Many of the items in this guest room I purchased at le Marché aux Puces. The mirror and the marble-topped console with its collection of Chinese lamps and French faience work beautifully together.

blue sky thinking

As a color scheme, blue and white works as well in a country setting as it does in a city loft. It's a combination that brings a sense of style to any interior, and I love using blue and white in unexpected ways. My home in Aspen is in a modern building from the sixties, but when one walks inside, it is like stepping into another world. I wanted to create the coziness of the chalets I remembered from my first visits to Switzerland.

In the master bedroom, a Swedish mirror, painted table, and topiary make a strong statement against a backdrop of upholstered walls in a blue cotton stripe.

A canopy creates a haven in this bedroom, and I love the play of the blue, white, and red floral pattern used on the bed with the blue striped fabric on the walls.

The master bedroom is decorated with antique Swedish furniture. The reproduction iron canopy bed faces out over an unimpeded view of the Roaring Fork River.

It is always the details that make the difference in a room. Filling the space

I love how all the reds, from the bowl of cherries to the mini-carnations and checked ribbons, complement the blue-and-white hues.

with things one loves establishes a warm and welcoming ambiance.

a splash of blue

For my bathroom, I chose pure white with blue accessories and the same fabric for the chairs and benches that I used in the bedroom. This gives the suite of rooms a comfortable flow, and while the bedroom is serene, the bath with its white walls, white marble, and blue accents always appears clean and fresh.

The focal point of the bathing area may be a portrait in a gilt-wood frame above the marble-topped tub, but blue and white makes a statement, too, in pieces of porcelain and as a trim on washcloths and towels.

When decorating, I carried the style and fabrics from the master bedroom into the bath and dressing area to create a flowing suite of rooms that belong together stylistically, even though they serve very different purposes.
Opposite: Over the fireplace is a George III mirror that seemed symbolic to me with its scrolled C at the top flanked by carved phoenixes—Carolyne rising from the ashes. The painted bench is nineteenth-century German.

A FIREPLACE BRINGS WARMTH AND BEAUTY INTO A room. The original Weatherstone had nine fireplaces, and when I rebuilt, I decided to add two more—one in the new central hall and the other in my bathroom. I loved the idea of a bubble bath with a glowing fire, a glass of champagne, soft lights, music, fluffy white towels, and a couple of my dogs snoozing on the bath mat—what bliss! All three master baths in my homes are much more than utilitarian places. As I prepare for the day or evening activities, I reflect on upcoming or recent events. I use this solitary time to collect my thoughts and always keep paper and pens nearby to jot notes and reminders.

Therefore I wanted this room to have the look and feel of a living space. A combination of French, English, and Swedish antiques and paintings makes the bath a pleasing place in which to greet the day or night and an inviting place for the pups to hang out with me. (There's always a bowl of fresh water next to the fireplace for them.)

I purchased these whimsical Italian chairs in Madrid many years ago. Fortunately they were in storage and not in the house at the time of the fire. I love painted furniture, and these chairs have their original eighteenth-century paint that works beautifully with my indigo fabric. Opposite: A close-up shows off the blue-and-white trims encircling the floral embroidery and the blue painted details on the chair.

A view of the dressing table with lily of the valley bouquets and a trio of perfume bottles in gold and blue glass. Opposite: The table faces south, and there is a lovely light that pours into the bath. The table is an early-nineteenth-century French painted piece from Provence; the chair, with a seat covered in a blue-and-white cut velvet, is eighteenth-century French.

in the bathroom

One of the charming aspects of the old Weatherstone was the double master baths that had been redone just after the turn of the twentieth century. Those were the days when ladies and gents did not share baths. The master bath was tiled in early Art Deco tiles in white, black, and burgundy, while the bath for the mistress of the house was tiled in blue and white.

A trio of robes, each found in different parts of the world, shows off the appealing reach of blue and white's influence. Opposite: In the master bath at the old Weatherstone, the walls were white, and blue and white stood out on the checkerboard floor, and in the antique blue tiles that bordered the room at the ceiling.

My love of blue and white, coupled with my desire for beautiful linens, makes

In the bath, left to right: Pretty embroidery in classic blue and white is equally appealing to both sexes. On an old washstand is everything needed to freshen up: A pitcher of water, a basin, creamy soap, and crisp towels. My linens come from all over: India, France, Italy, Portugal, and China. I love how the stripes, florals, and embroidered patterns reside beautifully next to each other.

it a pleasure to look for the decorative details that give this bath a finished look.

The pool at Weatherstone, with its nearby wisteria-covered pergola, is as much a spot for summer lunches as a place to swim or exercise. I wanted a simple shaded place where I could invite guests or simply sit and read or gaze at the garden.

For years I kept a picture of a pool that had been decorated with blue-and-white tiles and porcelain. When I added the simple pergola, I began to look for oversized blue-and-white porcelain with which to decorate my outdoor room. I was able to give my pool some of that flair with the large reproduction jardinières.

As we do not have the cool breezes of a beach house, the shaded pergola offers a

*The shaded seating area is a nice place to relax with a good book or,
as Lucky does, after a dip in the pool. Pillows with Moroccan tile motifs or
nautical stripes look fresh against the dark green summery ferns.*

reprieve from the intense summer sun for everyone, including all of my dogs.

Entertaining

Flowers and food look fabulous on
tables decorated with blue and white.
The endless assortment of dishes,
glassware, and linens available in
this bold combination enables the
hostess to create beautiful tables
for every season, occasion, and budget.

2

dining al fresco

The magic of blue and white is in its
endless variations and the fact that
practically all blues work together.
One can beautifully mix cerulean, indigo,
aqua, cobalt, sapphire, slate, Prussian,
cornflower, and navy to name just a few.
I suppose that is one of the reasons I have
collected so many different blues and whites
in dishes, as it allows me to create a vast
array of different tables for entertaining.

*A summer lunch is set in a corner on the veranda with a view over the
boxwood out to the formal herb garden behind the breakfast room.*

In Paris, there is a wonderful discount fabric emporium, Dreyfus, in Montmartre. There, I usually find a few meters of reasonably priced fabrics to use for one of my countless projects. This wonderful toile de Jouy in a camaïeux bleu has a creamy white background that's perfect with my creamware dishes and the warm white of the carnations. Aquamarine glasses pick up the light blue in this heavenly print.

A bit of history: In 1774, Josiah Wedgwood
perfected Jasperware, a fine stoneware with a
colored background decorated with classic bas-relief
figures based on Greek or Roman mythology.
Opposite: This toile resembles a painting technique
called camaïeux, which uses a single color (in this
case, cerulean) to depict a romanticized scene.

The moment the first warm rays of sun hit the terrace in late April, I move breakfast, lunch, and dinner into my outdoor room at Weatherstone. Blue and white lends a crisp, fresh note to any landscape and sets off associations with spring and summer and a return to sunny days spent in the open air.

*The veranda at Weatherstone is an outdoor room
that makes a graceful transition between the
actual house and the garden, an important factor
in landscape design. The blue-and-white theme
from the main house is echoed in the striped
cushion fabric for the outdoor seating areas.*

While the presentation is as detailed and formal as any of the dinners and parties I give within the house, the idea that we are finally outside adds a spirit of carefree relaxation—as if we're at an outdoor picnic.

My favorite elements for a table: a blue-and-white striped tablecloth, a mix of decorative pieces from my various blue-and-white collections of Delft, Chinese export porcelain, and Wedgwood; and the wonderful tree peonies from my garden.

I found this Sunbrella fabric in a classic stripe that works perfectly with my antique tableware, as well as the reproduction ginger jars and garden seats that decorate the veranda. Opposite: The bold stripes ground the prettier flourishes on the table, from the monogrammed napkin to the etched glasses.

When peonies are in season, I am inspired to do several lunches and dinners to celebrate their beauty. Blue and white is the perfect background to showcase the range of glorious pinks and reds of my favorite flowers. Opposite: Warm hues look glorious next to a piece of Delft.

A bold blue-and-white stripe I had made for a New York City ballet gala gets recycled into a cloth to dress a table on the porch of my studio. My favorite patterns are stripes of almost any scale. Their modern classicism allows them to work equally well in a traditional or contemporary setting. Opposite: Creamy roses and white phlox in hand-painted cobalt glasses soften the strong geometrics.

Whether for a benefit for eight hundred or a private

Warm Vegetable Terrine
Mâche and Arugula

Roasted Free Range Chicken
Tarragon Mustard Sauce
Purée of Pea and Watercress
Pommes Gaufrettes

Strawberry Rhubarb Cobbler
Green Tea Ice Cream

Carramar Estate Chardonnay 1999
Carramar Estate Merlot 1999

*When I created this look at home, flowers were cut from my garden
and the vases were etched cobalt glass. Reproducing the idea of that
table on a grand scale requires affordable flowers and table elements
that are mass-produced—like these silvery cups and tall white
candlesticks—but still give the same feeling as a lovely meal at home.*

dinner for eight, a blue-and-white theme looks spectacular.

Blue and white has always been a big part of my world, and this passion is reflected in the books I've done, whether the subject matter was flowers, entertaining, or creating beautifully wrapped gifts. I decided to include photos from my other books because each one makes a compelling case for falling in love with this classic combination.

While crisp and clean, the pairing of blue and white has the level of sophistication needed when putting exemplary pieces in an informal setting. Here, flowers in moss-filled fruit baskets play off the formality of the eighteenth-century chargers by British silversmith Paul Storr, Baccarat crystal, and early-nineteenth-century Regency decanters.

Prized for their tulips, the Dutch found an exquisite way of showing them off in a tulipier, a special kind of vase with many openings. These unusual pieces are not easy to find, but I've been lucky enough to find two of them in blue and white. Every shade of tulip sings out in this tower of power, from coral, rose, and orange to the striking dark and light blooms here.

On a day when the sun comes out and warms the terrace, I like to put together an impromptu lunch outdoors. I use this blue-and-white tulipier to make the table look special. When you have such a stunning piece, other elements should maintain a low profile, and extras—like a printed tablecloth—can be kept in the drawer.

My own version of tulipmania: These faience pyramids have a monumental impact, especially filled with white swan tulips and black and white parrot tulips. Opposite: Cobalt glasses, blue Canton boxes, and other reproduction pieces harmonize with the dramatic centerpiece.

On a hot summer day, billowing blue-and-white-checked

From At Home with Carolyne Roehm: *This picnic was inspired by a checked voile that I brought back from London and used to make a shade screen. Notice the mixing of different-sized checks and plaids.*

voile evokes the visual equivalent of a cool breeze.

Call it what you like—splatterware, graniteware, or pickleware—these blue-and-white tin enameled camp plates are the most stylish (and environmentally conscious) alternative to plastic or paper for an alfresco table. I like how fresh-picked strawberries and simple daisies pop against the classic blue-and-white American pattern.

Lunch is served: A hydrangea blue, white, and brown toile plays off the nineteenth-century French brown-and-white octagonal plates. The flowers match the fabric perfectly.

Hydrangeas dominate a blue-and-white-themed tabletop. Plates and tortoise-handled flatware beautifully contribute to the overall color scheme. Opposite: This delightful print is a surprising twist on the pastoral scenes normally associated with toile de Jouy.

a spring wedding

What could be prettier than a May
wedding done in blue and white?
The combination of these shades
has a freshness and innocence that
befits the occasion, whether it's held
at a beachside resort, on the grounds
of a country estate, or at a posh reception
space in New York City, like this one was.

*All of the details, from the white sweet peas to the sugar dragées, remained
true to the theme. Printed material, such as table numbers and tags for the
favors, was created on the computer in matching blue and white.*

WHEN A FRIEND ASKED me to help with her daughter's wedding, I immediately said yes. I love the idea of a blue-and-white reception in spring, and the French blue they had chosen was beautiful. The mother of the bride suggested an old-fashioned wedding luncheon, so we focused first on what the tables would look like. I discovered a source for classic vases in French blue to hold bouquets of spring flowers. Masses of white flowers—lilacs, lily of the valley, sweet peas, peonies, carnations, roses, and stock—filled various sizes and shapes of vases. No two tables were alike: I wanted the room to feel intimate, as if the family had summoned close friends to celebrate at their home rather than a big ballroom.

Brides still subscribe to the custom of "something old, something new, something borrowed, something blue," and this young woman particularly adored French blue. For her dress, the bride wore a beautiful Oscar de la Renta gown of embroidered white organdy with a blue satin sash, and her bridal bouquet held lily of the valley, a spring flower used on the luncheon tables as well.

A wedding is a time to go all out, but I love the way this one had a quiet sophistication. That comes from the elegant color scheme: French blue translates into a chic, cool hue next to a warm, creamy white, and all of the elements pay homage to that inspiration.

Clockwise from top left: Printed programs were edged with ribbon; even the domed ceiling in the Park Avenue ballroom fit the color scheme; quilted pillow boxes held sugar dragées. Wedding-favor boxes contained homemade sugar cookies embossed with the couple's initials (an idea I learned from Martha Stewart); blue satin ribbon and a cluster of white flowers brightened the gifts.

Often associated with faith, truth, and stability, blue is a

*The idea was to make it appear as if the mother of the bride had gone
into her garden to do the flowers for the party. We voted against an
over-the-top floral extravaganza and chose traditional spring blossoms
instead. The cake, designed by Sylvia Weinstock, followed suit, adding
sugar forget-me-nots, hydrangea, and spirea to the floral mix.*

lovely choice for a wedding, especially when married to white.

Breakfast in bed is a treat, but I like a table set at the foot of the bed rather than a morning tray, especially in this blue-and-white room in Paris (the honeymoon suite!) with its dramatic floral walls and striped canopy. Casual arrangements of white flowers nod in cobalt blue glasses; a blue-and-white gift beckons.

Blue and white works just as effectively as an accent. Just a

When strictly blue and white doesn't work for a bridal shower or birthday lunch, you can still inject it as a grace note to the overall scheme. Texture played a major role here: Pink blossoms reflect the embroidery on a silk taffeta tablecloth, while white linen napkins bear the Weatherstone cipher in blue—the same blue as the vintage silk poppies on gifts. A taffeta gingham bow and pink silk blossom provide a pretty flourish on an embossed gift box.

hint of it on a romantic pink table keeps the sweetness in check.

Entertaining in blue and white simplifies everything. This dynamic duo always looks fresh and appealing and works equally well in a modern or traditional setting. For a bridal shower, blue and white polka dots were all that was needed to set a perfect table. Gift-wrapped presents became part of the décor and a triple-tier cake held center stage.

MBM Nancy Berger

MBM Rod Newman

MARIA & MARK BINGHAM

WED

JUNE 28, 2007

MBM

Presentation is everything: Pretty place cards and a

Making the party scene, from left to right: These "engraved" place cards were done on my computer. Gold-rimmed Limoges plates hold a treat in a wrapped slide box for each guest. This magical cake by Sylvia Weinstock, which takes its cue from the dotted Swiss gift wrap, has a commanding presence; white roses and parrot tulips in sugar sit on the top tier. Mixing textures always makes a setting more interesting. A white dotted ribbon is subtle on a blue paper, whose texture resembles guipure lace.

wrapped gift at each table setting signify a good time to come.

From the Garden

White flowers abound, and glorious delphinium, hydrangeas, and bachelor buttons are the most brilliant blue blossoms. The way other colors from the garden pop when arranged in a blue-and-white vase makes it inspiring to create endless bouquets with surefire style and ease.

Blue is a constant presence in nature, from the sky above to the deep oceans below. What's curious is how few flowers come in blue, while all of the other colors, including white, have countless examples. Luckily, the ones that exist are truly glorious and provide numerous opportunities to create beautiful bouquets.

Flower lore points to the delphinium as a ward against lightning, and in Transylvania, the flower was thought to keep witches from stables because of its blue hue. Opposite: In a reproduction Chinese vase, however, these beautiful stems are striking in a wholly different way.

Hydrangeas in blue and white flirt next to white Brookside Snowball dahlias. Opposite: In a guest room at the old Weatherstone before the fire, blue and white was a stylistic element throughout, from the Oriental plates and Delft vases to the flower arrangements and ribbon-tied artwork. (Look closely at how blue larkspur and morning glories figure in the framed pictures.)

Rules of flower arranging often go out the window when I find something extraordinary in the garden, like these flowering branches. In truth, I really don't abide by rules, but instead try to do something new every time. Creating a vignette with different flowers is more interesting than a single bouquet.

The wild beauty of these prunus branches is anchored by the formality of the porcelain vases and cachepots. I brought other white flowers into play, including lily of the valley and gardenia. You can imagine how fragrant the room was with all of the bouquets.

Hydrangeas are one of my favorite kinds of flowers, especially in these appealing deep blues and periwinkles. Opposite: Bachelor buttons and white carnations delight the eye in a glossy pitcher; a linen napkin from Hungary picks up the color scheme in its border.

Bachelor Button

Larkspur

Forget-Me-Nots

Delphinium

Scabiosa

Scillia

Hydrangea

Delphinium

A mixed bouquet of
delphinium and blue and
purple lupin has accents
of white peonies to tie
in with the pattern on
the vase. Opposite: The
range of blues in flowers
goes from deep cornflower
to bluesy-lavender.

blue & white plus colors

Whenever you place any color next to blue and white, something magical occurs: All of a sudden, the focus sharpens and the visual field has clarity and power. You might argue that any hue paired with white does the same, but I beg to differ. (Black and white being the only exception!) Proof lies on the following pages, and I hope you'll be inspired to create your own magic with this combination.

I love how the subtle pinks in the anemones, cosmos, and roses pick up the warm hues on a blue-and-white piece of nineteenth-century transferware.

This is one of my favorite tables ever. While a mix of seventeenth-century Kangxi and eighteenth-century Delft elevates inexpensive modern reproductions, it's the luscious butter yellow, coral, and pink roses against the striped symmetry of blue and white that heightens the visual drama of the setting.

Peonies bloom for around three weeks, and during that time,
I take advantage of their sumptuous beauty. Here, a tree
peony with a vibrant yellow center plays a starring role in a
blue-and-white garlic vase. Opposite: A soft blue-and-white
damask tablecloth and vases filled with blue hydrangeas set
an exquisite stage to spotlight heavenly pink tree peonies.

When you want a particular flower to be the star of

an arrangement, blue and white acts as a fitting backdrop.

A mini-bouquet of colorful flowers from the garden includes tiny pansies and roses. Most blue-and-white linens favor the latter shade as the dominant one, but when I created this design, I reversed the emphasis with embroidered lily of the valley on what I like to call "Roehm" blue. Opposite: Pink cosmos and Japanese anemones look fresh and feminine in miniature reproduction vases.

Working with a riot of color takes a certain amount of fearlessness, but blue and white can be a calming influence in the adventure. When summer flowers explode in all their red, orange, pink, and yellow hues, their exuberant spirit inspires me to gather armfuls of them in a massive bouquet for an outdoor table. Even then it's not enough: Small, tight bouquets in terra-cotta pots sit at each place for guests to enjoy close up.

All the hot hues in this arrangement pop next to a classic blue-and-white-checked tablecloth, but pastels, mid-tones, and cool tones would look good too. For this luncheon, I used new windowpane-checked dishtowels for napkins and china that reflected the color scheme.

An ombré silk ribbon makes a
nosegay of pink roses noteworthy in a
hand-painted glass. Opposite: Even
when there's a mix of patterns, blue
and white unites the diversity, so a
gorgeous bunch of peonies stands out.

Summery bouquets of flowers in red and pink can be a bright

Singular sensations, left to right: Cockscomb and pinky-red carnations in an English Parian pitcher; a flotilla of peonies in vases of varying heights; Burma gem dahlias in a deep-blue pot; two shades of carnations in English transferware.

counterpoint to blue-and-white containers of every style.

Chinese blue-and-white
bowls on wooden pedestals
elevate begonias on a
window ledge framed with
curtains in a Provençal
print. Design note: A trio
of similar arrangements
is an effortless way to ensure
a strong visual statement.

Orange sits at the opposite side of the color spectrum from blue, but the sunny shade resides beautifully alongside blue-and-white elements at an alfresco luncheon. On both tables, a miniature orange tree creates a stylish centerpiece. Opposite: Bunches of paperwhite narcissus underscore the other white elements on a table accented with bowls of kumquats.

Painters play with shadings of light and dark, and I have learned a lot about balancing tonalities and patterns by contemplating their artistry. I've also discovered how home decoration should pay homage to a piece of art rather than trying to steal the limelight. Luckily, blue and white holds its own beautifully next to an English hunting painting.

Dahlia, viburnum berries, roses, and hypernicum hint at the golden sky in the oil painting, while the blue-and-white reproduction porcelain creates its own subtle landscape.

At Christmas, these blue-and-white pieces show off amaryllis, ilex berries, roses, and carnations. Opposite: In a warmer season, lavender hydrangeas and red roses secure a prominent place in the tableau.

A mahogany brown urn appears stately next to blue-and-white porcelain vases. Opposite: Almost every interior designer I know raves about the famous yellow drawing room created by Nancy Lancaster on Avery Row in London. Its rich buttercup yellow interior was the inspiration behind these walls at Weatherstone, which provide a warm backdrop for a row of porcelain.

blue & white

plus yellow

Nothing evokes summer like the
combination of blue, white, and yellow.
Painter Claude Monet understood
their sublime power and created
porcelain dinnerware in this
combination for his home at Giverny.
These strong primary colors call to mind
blue skies and brilliant sunshine, and
along with white, complement each
other in a breath-of-fresh-air way.

*Miniature sunflowers in cobalt blue American pressed glass
vases need no other adornment to make an appealing statement.*

Sunflowers reign from July through September, and the crowning point of my summer garden is when I'm able to gather masses of these bold and colorful blooms to produce great-looking tables in blue and white. Even the names of the sunflower varieties are stylish—sunbeam, Velvet Queen, Prado gold, and Fashion Mix.

Blue skies, fluffy white clouds, and a bright sunny sky: Spring brings daffodils and a chance to capture the reawakening of nature on a beautiful luncheon table. A blue-and-white matelassé tablecloth is set with reproduction Regency crystal, and small bouquets in blue-and-white vases enchant at each place setting.

One year I celebrated Easter in Paris, and after a long, gray stretch of winter, this blue-and-white table lifted my spirits. Bright daffodils ensured a cheerful mood, proving again how this energetic shade plays so well with blue and white. Opposite: Certain objects never lose their appeal. Year after year, I enjoy looking at the hand-painting on these handblown eggs from Hungary, and marvel at how perfect they look on English transferware.

Zinnia
"Canarybird"

Marigold
"Climax"

Sunflower
"Valentine"

Sunflower "Sonia"

Zinnia
"Tutti Mix Orange"

Sunflower
"Cream"

Coreopsis
"Bright Lights"

Rudbeckia
"Indian Summer"

Coreopsis
"Tinctoria"

I love brilliant sunshine-yellow flowers combined with cobalt blue glass. More than any other color combination, this says "summer" to me. Opposite: Sunflowers, marigolds, and zinnias project a sunny attitude that counters the coolness of blue.

Blue and white is calm and refreshing, and in their midst,

A never-fail formula, left to right: Bright yellow flowers such as chrysanthemums, daffodils and ranunculus, blue forget-me-nots and buttercups from the garden, and an autumnal crop of gold chrysanthemums succeed beautifully in blue-and-white containers.

a blaze of tantalizing yellow feels like a hit of sunshine.

Collecting

Blue and white is an artful color motif
evident in more cultures than any other.
The Chinese, Moors, Dutch, French,
English, Portuguese, Swedish, and Persian
cultures have created ceramics, textiles,
paints, and glass in myriad blues
with whites throughout history—
much to the delight of collectors like me.

collecting objects

I began "collecting" blue and white thirty-five years ago. I use the word *collecting* liberally as the only objects of any value I had at that time were two Blue Canton nineteenth-century plates. The rest of the objects decorating my blue-and-white apartment were found at a shop in Chinatown and in my travels. With my limited budget, my collecting was confined to reproductions that had a "look" rather than a provenance. My collection of blue and white has come a long way!

Light blue plates with navy insignia and monogram are French porcelain (Union Lumon Grandes Fabricant Paris) from the nineteenth century.

The bulk of my dinnerware collections are English—Wedgwood, English Stone china, Spode, and Wooster—and French Chantilly (opposite) from both the eighteenth and nineteenth centuries.

As a collector, I'm fascinated by how a particular plate reflects the life and times of the place where it was created. Many of the preeminent porcelain manufacturers throughout history were royal enterprises, and the enamel colors, rich border designs, and elaborate scenes and motifs on these plates often have a meaning beyond mere surface beauty.

I have collected blue-and-white plates since the seventies. My first prized piece was a single Blue Canton plate. Years later, my collection is a virtual United Nations of porcelain with French Chantilly, Sèvres, and Apt ware, as well as English Wedgwood, Spode, Wooster, English Ironstone and Stone china, Danish porcelain, and German Meissen pieces.

So many cultures and countries have a tradition of blue-and-white tableware, including faience from France and Meissen from Saxony. The teacups on these pages come from other sources: Royal Copenhagen porcelain from Denmark and Spode soft-paste porcelain from England.

Whether you set out to collect priceless antiques, reproductions, or a new design, it is such fun to build, edit, and upgrade a collection. A lot of the pleasure is in watching it grow and being able to relive when, where, and how you found the newest addition.

Each piece in my collection tells a story—not only the tale of where I found it, but also the history of its artistry. A trio of urns, left to right: Chinese-inspired Delft, late Delft with a Rococo influence, and nineteenth-century French faience. Bottom row: These nineteenth-century English pieces are beautiful examples of blue-and-white artistry.

MOST OF US want to collect objects that are beautifully made, esthetically pleasing, and also good investments. Learning about what makes an object great or valuable is interesting, but developing a good eye is invaluable when it comes to mixing old and new or high and low with style. In fact, style is about doing just that.

People often ask me how I learned to put things together. That is difficult to answer. But when pressed, I say it is a combination of things. I have spent my entire life looking and learning—this is natural to a designer. Everywhere I go—be it a stroll in the garden, a walk down Madison Avenue, or traipsing through a souk in Morocco, my eyes are always looking for what's unusual.

Blue and white gives me a focus—and it's a focus that's endlessly rewarding, because there are so many types of blue-and-white ceramics to explore. I am always looking for a good design or a memorable treasure. This insatiable desire to "see" coupled with years of exposure and study gave me the arsenal to create beautiful tabletops, decorate innumerable spaces, and plant many gardens over the years.

Many Chinese porcelain antiques in blue and white date back to the eighteenth and nineteenth centuries, the periods when the export trade was flourishing. Next to ivy topiaries in reproduction pots stand examples of these types of ceramics.

It's not surprising that I am drawn to blue-and-white porcelain: So many of the patterns include my favorite flowers—peonies and chrysanthemums. When the Dutch East India Company first brought Chinese porcelain to Europe, it was available only to royalty and the very wealthy. Delft potters began to copy and be inspired by the Chinese originals, making the look available to a wider audience.

Most of my collection of Delft is eighteenth century, but I do have some earlier, more valuable seventeenth-century pieces. I love spreading a line of Delft down a long table, especially when these pieces are matched with my favorite peonies or garden roses.

History shows even famous collections of blue and white combined cultures and eras. Notable among them is Queen Mary II of England's Delft-Ware Closet at Hampton Court with its walls filled with Dutch, Chinese, and Japanese pieces. I often mix my seventeenth- and eighteenth- century pieces with reproductions to great effect, especially on a dinner table.

If you were to create a timeline that marked innovations in ceramics, blue and white would always pop up. Historians point to its universal appeal, as well as the reliability of cobalt blue pigment, whose use dates back to ninth-century Middle Eastern ceramics. All of the objects pictured here are reproductions, except for the nineteenth-century transferware pitcher (top, right).

Adequate storage is vital for a large collection of old and new blue-and-white collectibles. These glass cupboards filled with all the different shapes and colors of blue also serve as pretty decoration in the breakfast room at Weatherstone.

cobalt glass

Blue is a color long associated with wealth and prosperity, so it seems fitting cobalt blue glassware was popular during the Depression: During difficult times, people gravitate to what provides solace and beauty, and cobalt blue reflects a purity and serenity that's appealing. But cobalt blue glass has a long, beautiful history, one that goes back to the eighteenth century and continues today.

A large early-nineteenth-century cobalt bowl holds my favorite blue flower—the hydrangea.

I use these antique bulb glasses as vases, slipping feminine white blossoms—narcissus, along with lemon leaves, white garden roses, and lisianthus—in the cobalt blue vessels. Opposite: One year, I hosted New Year's Eve in my greenhouse at Weatherstone, and chose blue and white as a color palette instead of the traditional reds and greens of Christmas.

Originally cobalt was a precious component in paint, but its deep-as-the-ocean hue quickly found its way onto porcelain and glassware. Alongside English transferware and export china, I've collected etched crystal and cobalt glass and like to mix modern pieces with treasured antiques. *Opposite: Silver is a cool counterpoint to blue-and-white pieces on a tabletop.*

Clear as a bell: Blue is the unifying theme in my collection of glass bells, which come in all different heights and patterns with simple or ornate handles. While I suppose you might use one of them to summon guests to dinner (yes, each has its own little clanker), they serve mostly to delight the eye with their intense color and pleasing shapes.

You might think these glass bells are Venetian, but they are actually English and date back to the nineteenth century. When I found the collection at James Robinson antiques in Manhattan, I couldn't resist their whimsical beauty.

History reveals that blown-glass vessels date back to the first century, but it wasn't until the late 1600s that glassmakers understood how to achieve a more crystalline, softer glass that could be etched, cut, or ground. The art of making crystal glassware had its origins in England, but found its way to glassmaking centers in Italy, Ireland, Czechoslovakia, Bavaria, and France. My cobalt collection has an international provenance.

blue & white Linens

My love of beautiful linens is deep-seated and began back in Missouri, where my Grandmother Beatty would go to estate sales looking for antiques, and would frequently return with lovely old table and bed linens made from heavy damask or Irish linen, often embroidered with beautiful designs.

Clean, crisp, classic: This collection of blue-and-white napkins and hand towels comes from Hungary, Portugal, Greece, France, and other sources closer to home.

A sweet bouquet of lily of the valley complements these blue linen napkins that I designed with an embroidered motif of my birth flower. I prefer oversized twenty-four-inch squares for dinner and twenty-two-inch squares for luncheon.

Corrine Albert

The Italians, French, Irish, Belgians, and Portuguese have long-established traditions for creating beautiful linens. Fortunately a few firms in America are making our own lovely designs by importing material from one of the above-mentioned countries.

Blue and white is never, ever fussy. That's probably one of the reasons it's universally appealing to men and women, making it a useful color combination when setting a beautiful table or preparing a guest room. It doesn't overwhelm the senses, offend no-nonsense personalities, or act as a distraction with showier elements.

Embroidered linens, whether they are in cotton or real linen, are truly a luxury, because they require special care. But what a difference they make when beautifully ironed on a table or bed. That is real luxury!

papers
& ribbons

While I love many, many colors and
have stationery, papers, and ribbons
in just about every color in the rainbow,
the predominant theme of my paper stash
is still blue and white. Pretty notepads, gift
wrap, cards, and writing implements in various
shades of the combination are in the guest
bedrooms and fill my desks in my homes.

*A simple striped gift wrap, blue cotton ribbon, and a cluster
of daisies are great decoration for any spring or summer gift.*

I've collected blue-and-white papers and ribbons for many years, so I love to put together new combinations like this floral paper and woven striped ribbon. Opposite: A close-up of these hand-blocked Italian papers reveals their beauty.

Engraved invitations on beautiful card stock are a luxury for formal or special occasions, and I love choosing just the right typeface to reflect the theme. But there's something equally satisfying about how my favorite fonts are available on my computer, making it easy to prepare menu cards, gift tags, or placecards at a moment's notice.

Since blue and white is my signature color combination, I have stationery that reflects my interest. (Note the blue paper clips!) For dinner parties, it's fun to print up menu cards on my computer: Guests feel as if you've taken the time to create something special, and when the colors correspond to the party décor—especially if it's blue and white—you truly have.

Celebrating Spring
Please join Carolyne
for
lunch in the daffodils
at
Weatherstone

April 5th 2007
at Six O'clock

...ingham

Baby blue and white is a sweet combination that benefits from

*Robin's egg blue and white is a sweet spring
combination that becomes more sophisticated when
combined with a vibrant yellow and olive green.*

notes of unexpected color such as butter yellow or olive green.

While blue and white works for every season on a table or in home décor, the combination feels inherently cheerful on gift wrap, especially in the lighter blue tonalities of these hand-blocked patterns. Opposite: I stamped carnations in Delft blue on white freezer paper for this pretty package.

Navy and white is probably my favorite pairing, thanks in part to Coco Chanel, who understood how sophisticated these two colors look together. For a bridal shower luncheon, I took a classic approach to the color scheme and tied disparate elements together in navy and white. The result? A pretty setting that feels formal, but not fussy.

Saddle-stitched ribbon, polka-dots, stripes, and Chanel's signature flower, the camellia, provide texture and visual interest to the navy and white party décor. The individual mini-cakes dreamed up by Sylvia Weinstock were topped with sugar lily of the valley, and were inspired by my classic navy saddle-stitched ribbon.

Elements & Inspiration

A swatch of fabric from France initiated
me into the world of design possibilities
associated with blue and white.
Thus began a lifelong interest in the
way this wonderful combination enlivens
everything from napkins and drapes
to wrapping paper and ribbons.

fabrics & trims

My interest in textiles was instilled at a very young age by my grandmother, but it became a passion when I began working as a design assistant to Oscar de la Renta and was exposed to the range of beautiful fabrics from the famous European textile houses. When I began my own business and started to decorate my various homes, wonderful fabrics and trims became a primary source of inspiration for fashion and home alike.

Italy and France are fabulous sources for extraordinary fabrics and passementerie, supplying both the fashion and interior design industries. This is a classic pattern from the Italian textile firm Branchini. See how the texture of the tassels mixes beautifully with the design of the fabric.

champion cobalt

deep royal

W|4b
2061-10

This English crewel (Lee Jofa's Sohil Stripe) is one
of my favorites, and mixing it with a bold stripe
(opposite, Duralee's Pakistan Stripe) modernizes
this traditional fabric. The silk taffeta (Lee Jofa's
Oceana) and slate blue wool flannel pick up the
colors from the crewel stitching as do the paint chips
and trims (Samuel & Sons' Elysee border).

There are endless examples of fabrics in blue and white; these are a few of my personal favorites. Mixing florals with graphic patterns is always an effective way to create an exciting palette. Classics such as this toile, chinoiserie pattern, and an adaptation of an ikat are all wonderful designs that have stood the test of time.

Center, top: Brunschwig et Fils' Verriers is a glazed chintz named after the chateau at Verrières-le-Buisson, home of French woman of letters Louise Levêque de Vilmorin. This was the beautiful fabric I longed to use in my first apartment and plan to use in my next project. Shown (center, bottom) with Old World Weavers' Trianon stripe, and trims from Samuel & Sons—Boucher's cross-weave braid and bell fringe. Left, top: Clarence House trim, Old World Weavers' Trianon stripe, Brunschwig & Fils' West Indies Toile (also shown below). Right, bottom: Brunschwig & Fils' Love Birds print mixes beautifully (above) with Cowtan & Tout's Karlsen stripe, a slate blue wool flannel, Samuel & Sons' Orsay silk ribbed border, and Clarence House's brush fringe.

When designing clothes, I always created a collection based on the fabrics I had selected; the same holds true for the rooms I have done. I put together a storyboard with the furniture, fabrics, and paint colors to serve as a map for the creative process. This is an important design discipline that helps me think on paper and avoid costly mistakes.

I choose a key fabric for a room and then find fabrics, trim, and paint colors that play a supporting role to that fabric. Left: Pierre Frey's Monuments de París (bottom) pairs with Cowtan & Tout's Matelasse stripe, Lee Jofa's Oceana taffeta, and Samuel & Sons' Elysee ribbed border and scalloped tassel fringe (top). Center, top: A botanical (Flora Danica) from Clarence House. Bottom: Cowtan & Tout's Indienne Voile matches up with Samuel & Sons' Orsay ribbed border and Annecy gimp. Right: A blue-and-white floral print (bottom, Brunschwig & Fils' Shell Toile) is the basis for a classic grouping (top) of stripes, plaid checks, and solid blue ottoman. Note how beautifully they combine with the range of hues on a Benjamin Moore paint strip.

blue & white paint

Paint is one of the easiest ways to change the look and feel of a room. Selecting the right color for your space and design requires knowledge and the willingness to experiment. Paint can be tricky: It is one thing when wet, another when dry, and the type of finish impacts on the color. Also, a paint color changes with different exposures of light.

There is an endless spectrum of white paints, which is what makes working with an all-white palette challenging. When one learns to create shadow and light with different shades of white paint, the degree of sophistication in a room increases dramatically.

winter white

2140-70

203

TALLOW

DIMITY

2008

1B | W

2142-70

snowfall white

1B | ● | W

1B | W

2144-60

ALL WHITE   2005

POINTING   2003

JAMES WHITE   2010

WHITE TIE   2002

CLUNCH   2009

BLACKENED   2011

W
INT. RM

white dove

C
INT. RM

atrium white

W
INT. RM

antique white

1170
Tawny Mist

2122-70

snow white

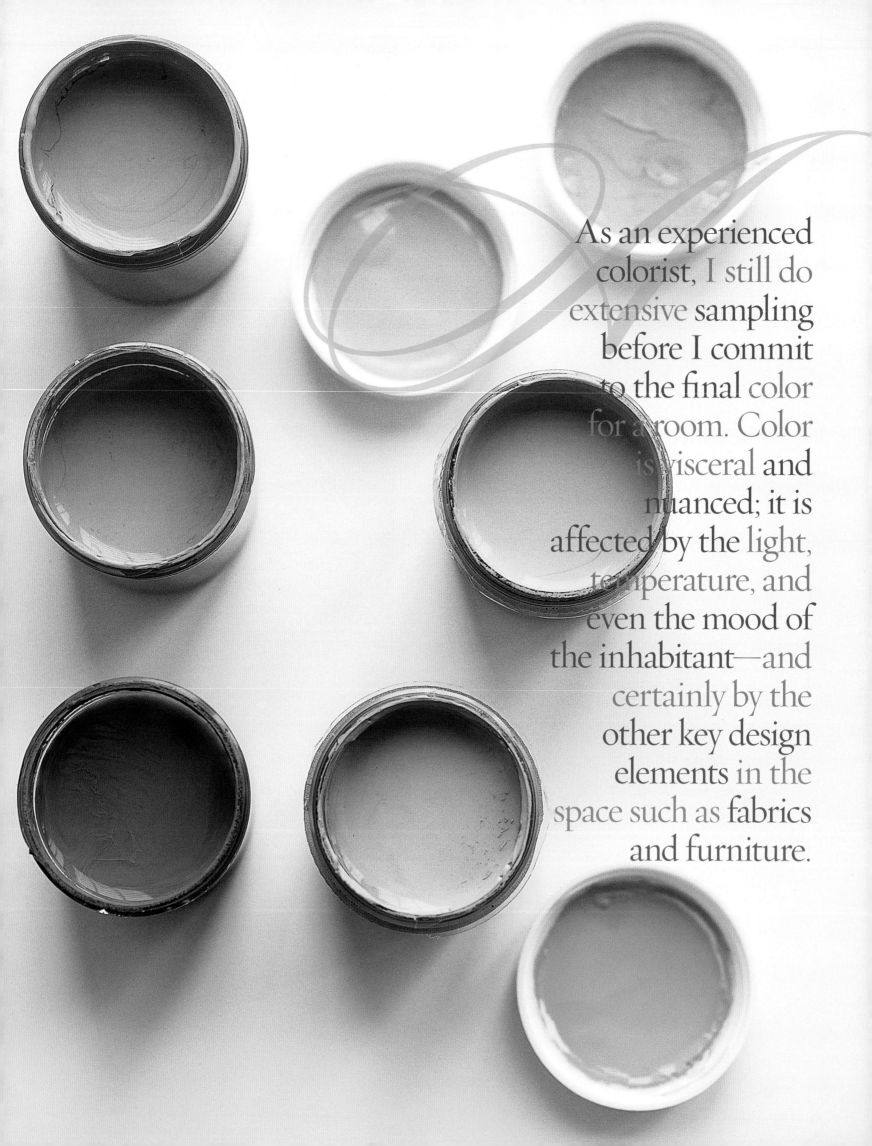

As an experienced colorist, I still do extensive sampling before I commit to the final color for a room. Color is visceral and nuanced; it is affected by the light, temperature, and even the mood of the inhabitant—and certainly by the other key design elements in the space such as fabrics and furniture.

white satin

W ● IB
2067

windmill wings

summer blue

PARMA GRAY® 27

W IB
2067-50

blue lapis

LULWORTH
BLUE 89

HACIENDA BLUE • SF17A

MOUNTAIN ICE • NZ04A

W 2B
2067-40

twilight blue

STONE BLUE 86

W 3B
2067-30

starry night blue

2067-

W IB
2062-60

CHINESE BLUE 90

blue hydrangea

midnight navy

W P-300 4B
2067-10

COOK'S BLUE 237

SOUTHAMPTON BLUE

blue jean

REFLECTING POOL • RH02A

PITCH BLUE 220

7231 P

blue daisy

Parlor Blue

7232 T

Early blue paints were expensive as they were
made from lapis and ground cobalt glass.
Fortunately today we have endless options to
choose from, and the advent of the computer
allows us to match any color we want.

inspiration comes from everywhere

If I had to say what inspires me, I would say "everything." When pressed, I would say my biggest sources of inspiration come from three areas: from Mother Nature, in the form of flowers and trees; from color, in nature (blue skies, snowflakes) or in man-made sources (beautiful ribbons and fabrics); and finally, from pattern—on textiles, prints on paper, and designs on china of all sorts.

My passion for blue and white is shared by artists from the past and present who add to the repertoire of this color combination, from Wedgwood pieces to stripes and toiles from Brunschwig & Fils, Pierre Frey, and Cowtan & Tout.

When I mix fabrics and other objects, I look for a common thread among the elements. That may be a color, or the juxtaposition of color and white space. Large patterns often need small-scale patterns to anchor them. I like the look of a toile and ikat (Brunschwig & Fils' Hampton Resist) with the marbled Apt ware plate or a piece of Wooster china (opposite) with a Clarence House Delft Blue linen and cotton.

Creating a story or the look of a collection of clothes, the design of a room, the decoration of a tabletop for a party, or the layout of a garden is a process beginning with an inspiration. That idea creates the concept, and then the selection of patterns, colors, textures, and styles follow to support and convey the concept.

For me, the mixing of patterns, colors, and texture is an endless source of fascination—and juxtaposing beautiful printed fabrics with a mix of china patterns shows the timelessness of blue and white.

sources

Once you become attuned to blue and white, you see it everywhere. This list is composed of some of my favorite places to find pieces, either antique or brand new. On my website, www.carolyneroehm.com, I have a whole section devoted to this classic color combination which I hope you'll find helpful.

ANTIQUES
Bardith, Ltd.
901 Madison Avenue
New York, NY 10021
212-737-3775
www.bardith.com

Charlotte Moss New York
20 East 63rd Street
New York, NY 10021
212-308-3888
www.charlottemoss.com

Chinese Porcelain Company
475 Park Avenue
New York, NY 10022
212-838-7744
www.chineseporcelain.com

Christie's
20 Rockefeller Plaza
New York, NY 10020
212-636-2000
www.christies.com

Dawn Hill Antiques
11 Main Street
New Preston, CT 06777
860-868-0066
www.dawnhillantiques.com

Doyle New York
Auctioneers & Appraisers
175 East 87th Street
New York, NY 10128
212-427-2730
www.doylenewyork.com

Elise Abrams Antiques
11 Stockbridge Road
Great Barrington, MA 01230
413-528-3201
www.eliseabrams.com

Guinevere Antiques
574-580 Kings Road
London SW6 2DY
+44(0) 207-736-8267
www.guinevere.co.uk

James Robinson Inc.
480 Park Avenue
New York, NY 10022
212-752-6166
www.jrobinson.com

John Rosselli International
523 East 73rd Street
New York, NY 10021
212-772-2137
www.johnrosselli.com

Manhing Imports
240 Fifth Avenue
New York, NY 10001
212-684-5090

Mallett Antiques
929 Madison Avenue
New York, NY 10021
212-249-8783
www.mallettantiques.com

Marche Paul Bert
96, Rue des Rosiers-18
93400 Saint Ouen
01-40-115-414

Sotheby's
1334 York Avenue
New York, NY 10021
212-606-7000
www.sothebys.com

Susan Silver Antiques
RR 7
Sheffield, MA 01257
413-229-8169

Treillage Limited
418 East 75th Street
New York, NY 10021
212-535-2288
www.treillageonline.com

NEW
ABC Carpet & Home
888 & 881 Broadway
New York, NY 10003
212-473-3000
www.abchome.com

Bergdorf Goodman
745 Fifth Avenue
New York, NY 10019
800-558-1855
www.bergdorfgoodman.com

Crate and Barrel
650 Madison Avenue
New York, NY 10022
212-308-0011
www.crateandbarrel.com

Fishs Eddy
889 Broadway
New York, NY 10003
212-420-9020
www.fishseddy.com

Pottery Barn
127 East 59th Street
New York, NY 10022
917-369-0050
www.potterybarn.com

Tiffany & Company
725 Fifth Avenue
New York, NY 10022
212-755-8000
www.tiffany.com

William-Wayne & Co.
850 Lexington Avenue
New York, NY 10022
212-737-8934
www.william-wayne.com

Williams-Sonoma
121 East 59th Street
New York, NY 10022
917-369-1131
www.williams-sonoma.com

FABRICS AND TRIMS
Most of the fabric houses in the
Decorators and Designers building
have blue and white fabrics and trims.
These are the ones I use in the D & D
Building, 979 Third Avenue,
New York, NY 10022:

Brunschwig & Fils
212-838-7878
www.brunschwig.com

Chelsea Textiles
212-319-5804
www.chelseatextiles.com

Clarence House
212-752-2890
www.clarencehouse.com

Country Swedish
212-838-1976
www.countryswedish.com

Cowtan & Tout
212-753-6511
www.cowtanandtout.com

Hinson & Company
212-688-5538

Lee Jofa
212-688-0444
www.leejofa.com

Old World Weavers
212-333-7186

Pierre Deux
212-644-4891
www.pierredeux.com

Pierre Frey (also has Branchini)
212-421-0534
www.pierrefrey.com

MORE TEXTILE SOURCES
Baranzelli
942 Third Avenue
New York, NY 10022
212-753-6511
www.baranzelli.com

Bennison Fabrics
The Fine Arts Building
232 East 59th Street
New York, NY 10022
212-223-0373
www.bennisonfabrics.com

Carlton V
Represented in the United States at
Design Diva Fabrics showroom
1855 North Central Expressway
Plano, TX 75075
972-423-4224
www.designdivafabrics.com

Dreyfus Déballage du Marché Saint
Pierre
2 Rue Charles Nodier
75018 Paris
01-46-06-92-25
www.marche-saint-pierre.fr

George Le Manach
Represented in the United States by
Claremont Inc.
Art and Design Building
1059 Third Avenue
New York, NY 10021
212-486-1252

Samuel & Sons Passementerie
983 Third Avenue
New York, NY 10022
212-704-8000
www.samuelandsons.com

Scalamandre
222 East 59th Street
Suites 110/210/310
New York, NY 10022
212-980-3888
www.scalamandre.com

AS WITH ALL OF MY OTHER BOOKS, *A Passion for Blue & White* is a collective effort on the parts of many people who have been a part of my book team for years. I wish to thank all of you for your continued hard work, advice, and above all else your talent and your belief in mine!

To my friend Sylvie Becquet, who has done 98 percent of the beautiful photography—thank you for your talent, hard work, and friendship.

To Alan Richardson and Mick Hales for your photographic contributions.

To the Weatherstone staff, Placido and Margarida de Carvalho, Vicky Morrel, and Nancy Quantrini, for their endless help and support.

To my "Gal Friday" Rosa Costa, who helps me in so many ways, checking, sourcing, ordering flowers, taking care of film, and generally making my life much easier in the process.

To the publishing and editing ladies who make sure I am on time and make coherent text out of my rambling prose. Thank you Donna Bulseco, Jennifer Josephy at Broadway Books, and my agent Cullen Stanley.

A special thank you to Doug Turshen and David Huang. I think this layout is your best yet! I know this will be one of my favorite books because of your design talent.

To the people I love who are always a support—Mom, Mittie Ann, and darling Simon.

I wish to thank all the people around the world who have collected my previous books for your support, for the kind words in your many letters and e-mails, and for always asking, "When will the new book be ready?" Well, here it is—book number 9. I hope you have enjoyed it!

All photographs were taken by Sylvie Becquet with the exception of the following pages:
Oberto Gigli: 84 (right), 85 (left)
Mick Hales: 177, 243
Alan Richardson: 81, 82, 83, 170, 171, 172, 173, 179, 185, 220, 221
Carolyne Roehm: 11 (right), 32–33, 130–131, 160–161, 162–163, 164–165, 184, 186–187, 224–225, 228–229, 250–251, 260–261, 264–265
Victor Skrebneski: 11 (left)

BROADWAY

Library of Congress Cataloging-in-Publication Data
Roehm, Carolyne.
  A passion for blue & white / Carolyn Roehm.
    p. cm.
  ISBN 978-0-7679-2113-8 (hardcover)
1. Blue in interior decoration. 2. White in interior decoration.
I. Title. II. Title: Passion for blue and white.
  NK2115.5.C6R64 2008
  747'.94—dc22

2008062315

10 9 8 7 6 5 4 3 2 1

First Edition

Printed in China